Pre-Raphaelite Cats

Pre-Raphaelite Cats

Susan Herbert

Thames & Hudson

A Pet

after Walter Howell Deverell

The keeping of caged birds was an
extremely popular Victorian practice.

Flora

after Evelyn de Morgan

The goddess of blossoms
and flowers.

Beata Beatrix

after Dante Gabriel Rossetti

After the death of his wife, Elizabeth
Siddel, from an overdose of laudanum,
Rossetti painted her as Beatrice, the ideal
love of Dante. The figures in the
background represent Dante and Love.

Claudio and Isabella

after William Holman Hunt

Claudio has been condemned to death by Angelo, the
Duke of Vienna's deputy. When Isabella pleads with
Angelo to spare her brother's life, Angelo agrees to set
Claudio free on condition that she will sleep with him.
Isabella feels sure that Claudio will gladly die rather than
allow this to happen and nervously awaits her brother's
reaction to Angelo's proposal.

" Dost thou think, Claudio,
  If I would yield him my virginity
  Thou mightst be freed"

(Shakespeare, *Measure for Measure*, Act III, Scene I)

Ecce Ancilla Domini

(the Annunciation)

after Dante Gabriel Rossetti

The archangel Gabriel appears
before the Virgin Mary.

Home from Sea

after Arthur Hughes

A young sailor, returning from the sea, weeps on the grave of his mother who died during his absence. His sister looks on sympathetically.

Isabella and the Pot of Basil

after William Holman Hunt

In Keats's poem, Isabella's unpleasant
brothers murdered her lover Lorenzo.
Heartbroken, she has concealed his head
in a pot of basil and embraces it passionately.

King Cophetua and the Beggar Maid

after Sir Edward Burne-Jones

"Bare-footed came the beggar maid
  Before the King Cophetua.
  In robe and crown the king stept down,
  To meet and greet her on her way;
  'It is no wonder,' said the lords,
  'She is more beautiful than day'."

(Tennyson, *The Beggar Maid*)

La Ghirlandata

after Dante Gabriel Rossetti

One of several paintings by Rossetti of
musical women in an aesthetic setting.

Mariana

after Sir John Everett Millais

Having lost her dowry in a shipwreck, Mariana
is abandoned by her lover Angelo and spends
the next five years in a moated grange.

(Shakespeare, *Measure for Measure*, and Tennyson, *Mariana*)

Musica (Melody)

after Kate Elizabeth Bunce

Representing the spirit of music.

Medea

after Frederick Sandys

Medea the enchantress assembles her various
symbols and prepares the ingredients for a spell.

Monna Vanna

after Dante Gabriel Rossetti

Monna Vanna is a character from
Dante's *Vita Nuova*

Ophelia

after John William Waterhouse

Rejected by Hamlet and devastated
by the murder of her father, Ophelia
loses her reason and drowns.

(Shakespeare, *Hamlet*, Act IV, Scene VII)

Princes in the Tower

after Sir John Everett Millais

After the death of their father King Edward IV, Edward, Prince of Wales, and his younger brother Richard, Duke of York, are imprisoned by their uncle in the Tower.

Psyche

after John William Waterhouse

Overcome by curiosity, Psyche opens the box
from Hades, which contains the spirit of sleep.

Regina Cordium

after Dante Gabriel Rossetti

The Queen of Hearts: a young woman
surrounded by emblems of love.

The Sleeping Princess

after Sir Edward Burne-Jones

Princess Aurora lies in the sleep
to which she was condemned for
a hundred years by the wicked
fairy who was not invited to
her christening.

The Awakening Conscience

after William Holman Hunt

A young woman, who has been living with a man out of wedlock, has a sudden revelation. Her lover, however, is as yet unaware that she has seen the sinfulness of her situation.

The Black Brunswicker

after Sir John Everett Millais

A young officer bids his fiancée a sad farewell
on the eve of the Battle of Waterloo.

The Blind Girl

after Sir John Everett Millais

A blind girl and her younger companion rest
in a field as they wait for the rain to pass.

The Bower Meadow

after Dante Gabriel Rossetti

A painting with no references, except
to show women with musical instruments
in an imaginary medieval background.

The Daydream

after Dante Gabriel Rossetti

"Within the branching shade of Reverie
  Dreams even may spring till autumn; yet none be
  Like woman's budding day-dream spirit-fann'd.
  Lo! tow'rd deep skies, not deeper than her look,
  She dreams; till now on her forgotten book
  Drops the forgotten blossom from her hand."

(Rossetti)

The Golden Stairs

after Sir Edward Burne-Jones

Though not based on any historical
or literary theme, this painting appears
to be a celebration of music, as many
of the figures carry musical instruments.

The Huguenot

after Sir John Everett Millais

In an attempt to save the life of her Huguenot
lover, a young girl tries to persuade him
to wear the white armband which would
identify him as a Catholic.

The Light of the World

after William Holman Hunt

"Behold, I stand at the door, and knock: if any man
hear my voice, and open the door, I will come in to
him, and will sup with him, and he with me."

(*Revelation*, III, 20)

The Mirror of Venus

after Sir Edward Burne-Jones

Venus and her handmaidens study
their reflections in a mystical pool.

The Long Engagement

after Arthur Hughes

These rather forlorn lovers have been
engaged for so long that ivy now covers
the tree where they carved their names.

The Proscribed Royalist

after Sir John Everett Millais

In the period of the English Civil War,
Elvira, a young woman allied to the
Roundheads, has a secret assignation
with her lover, Arturo, who is a Cavalier.

(Bellini, the opera *I Puritani*)

Veronica Veronese

after Dante Gabriel Rossetti

"Suddenly leaning forward, the Lady Veronica
rapidly wrote the first notes on the virgin page.
Then she took the bow of the violin to make her
dream reality; but before commencing to play
the instrument suspended from her hand, she
paused for a few moments, listening to the
inspiring bird, while her left hand strayed over the
strings searching for the supreme melody, still
elusive. It was the marriage of the voices of nature
and of the soul – the dawn of a mystic creation."

(Swinburne)

Original Paintings

p.2 **Flora**
Evelyn de Morgan
(The De Morgan Foundation, London)

p.5 **A Pet**
Walter Howell Deverell
(Tate Gallery, London)

p.7 **Beata Beatrix**
Dante Gabriel Rossetti
(Tate Gallery, London)

p.9 **Claudio and Isabella**
William Holman Hunt
(Tate Gallery, London)

p.11 **Ecce Ancilla Domini**
Dante Gabriel Rossetti
(Tate Gallery, London)

p.12-13 **Home from Sea**
Arthur Hughes
(Ashmolean Museum, Oxford)

p.15 **Isabella and the Pot of Basil**
William Holman Hunt
(Laing Art Gallery, Newcastle)

p.17 **King Cophetua and the Beggar Maid**
Sir Edward Burne-Jones
(Tate Gallery, London)

p.19 **La Ghirlandata**
Dante Gabriel Rossetti
(GuildhallArt Gallery, Corporation of London)

p.21 **Mariana**
Sir John Everett Millais
(The Makins Collection)

p.23 **Musica**
Kate Elizabeth Bunce
(Birmingham City Museums and Art Gallery)

p.25 **Medea**
Frederick Sandys
(Birmingham City Museums and Art Gallery)

p.27 **Monna Vanna**
Dante Gabriel Rossetti
(Tate Gallery, London)

p.29 **Ophelia**
John William Waterhouse
(Private Collection. Photo Christie's Images, London)

p.31 **Princes in the Tower**
Sir John Everett Millais
(Royal Holloway and Bedford New College, University of London)

p.33 **Psyche**
John William Waterhouse
(Private Collection)

p.35 **Regina Cordium**
Dante Gabriel Rossetti
(Glasgow Museum and Art Gallery)

p.36-37 **The Sleeping Princess**
(Briar Rose series)
Sir Edward Burne-Jones
(Faringdon Collection Trust, Buscot Park)

p.39 **The Awakening Conscience**
William Holman Hunt
(Tate Gallery, London)

p.41 **The Black Brunswicker**
Sir John Everett Millais
(National Museums & Galleries on Merseyside, Lady Lever Art Gallery)

p.43 **The Blind Girl**
Sir John Everett Millais
(Birmingham City Museums and Art Gallery)

p.45 **The Bower Meadow**
Dante Gabriel Rossetti
(Manchester City Art Galleries)

p.47 **The Daydream**
Dante Gabriel Rossetti
(Victoria & Albert Museum, London)

p.49 **The Golden Stairs**
Sir Edward Burne-Jones
(Tate Gallery, London)

p.51 **The Huguenot**
Sir John Everett Millais
(The Makins Collection)

p.53 **The Light of the World**
William Holman Hunt
(Keble College, Oxford)

p.54-55 **The Mirror of Venus**
Sir Edward Burne-Jones
(Gulbenkian Foundation, Lisbon)

p.57 **The Long Engagement**
Arthur Hughes
(Birmingham City Museums and Art Gallery)

p.59 **The Proscribed Royalist**
Sir John Everett Millais
(Private Collection)

p.61 **Veronica Veronese**
Dante Gabriel Rossetti
*(Delaware Art Museum.
Samuel and Mary R. Bancroft Memorial)*

SUSAN HERBERT is one of the most distinctive contemporary cat artists. Her work has been exhibited in theatres and galleries from London to Tokyo, and published in books including *Shakespeare Cats* and *Movie Cats*, also published by Thames & Hudson.

Pre-Raphaelite Cats © 1999
Thames and Hudson Ltd, London

First published in hardcover in the United States of America in 1999 by Thames and Hudson Inc., 500 Fifth Avenue, New York, New York 10110

thamesandhudsonusa.com

First paperback edition 2014

Library of Congress Catalog Card Number 98-75343

ISBN 978-0-500-29138-2

Printed and bound in China by Toppan Leefung Printing Limited